COPYRIGHT © 2022
St Shenouda Press

All rights reserved. No part of this book may be reproduced in any manner without prior written permission from the publisher.

ST SHENOUDA PRESS
8419 Putty Rd,
Putty, NSW, 2330
Sydney, Australia

www.stshenoudapress.com

ISBN 13: 978-0-6451395-1-8

Long ago, there lived a girl named Marina, she was born to a rich Christian family. When Marina was just a little girl, her mother passed away and she was left to live with her father. Her father was a good man, he was patient and caring. He knew that children are a beautiful blessing from God, he taught Marina everything about Jesus and the Bible. He was so happy to see that his daughter was walking in the footsteps of Jesus and learning the virtue of obedience, one of the most important virtues in life.

Years passed and Marina became a young lady. Her father dreamt of becoming a monk and living in a monastery where he could continue to serve God.

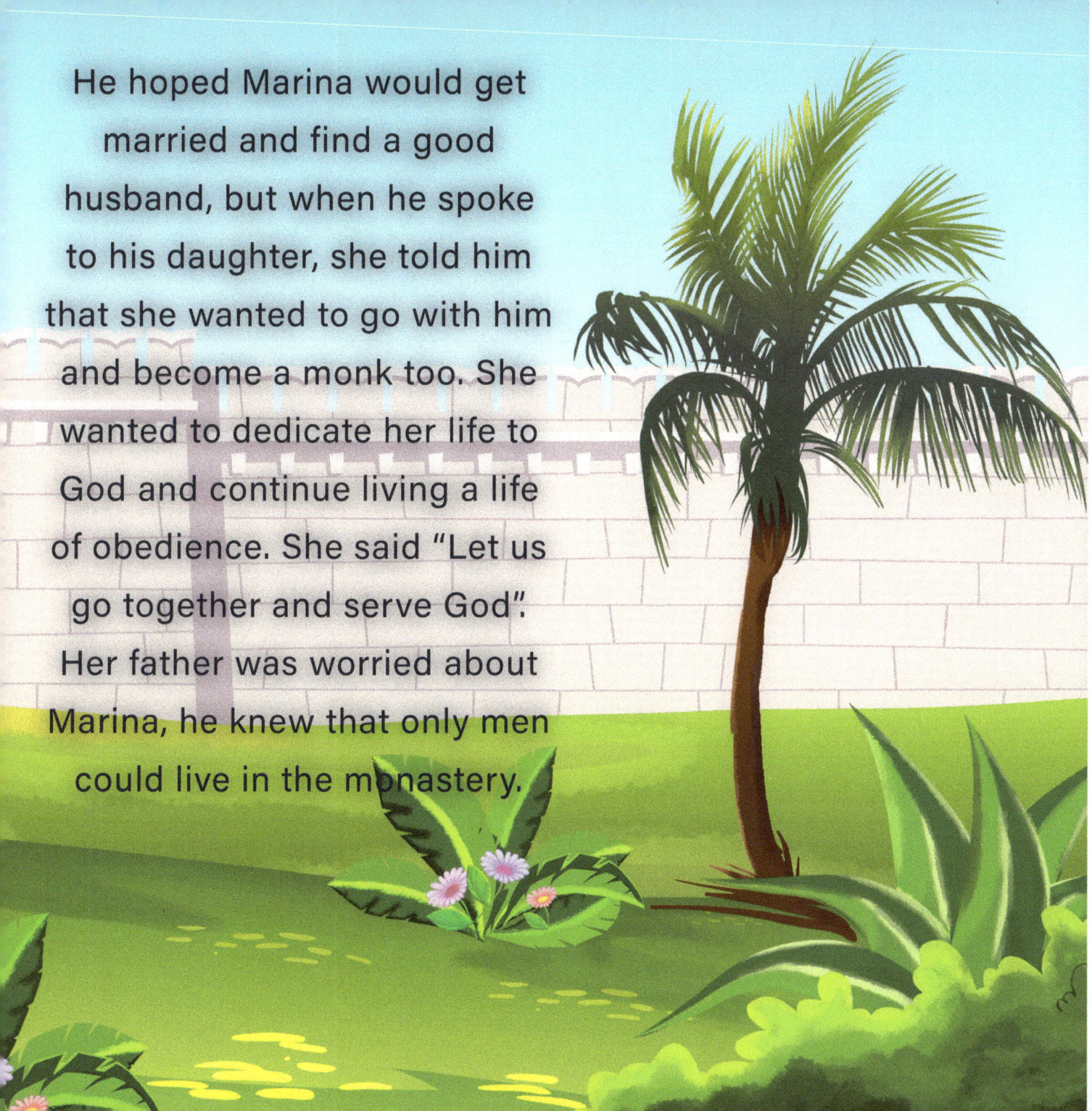

He hoped Marina would get married and find a good husband, but when he spoke to his daughter, she told him that she wanted to go with him and become a monk too. She wanted to dedicate her life to God and continue living a life of obedience. She said "Let us go together and serve God". Her father was worried about Marina, he knew that only men could live in the monastery.

Marina wanted to prove that she was not afraid, so without hesitation she rushed to her room, cut her long hair, took off her dress and put on one of her father's tunics. She loved God so much, she could feel His mighty call and was willing to do anything to join her father at the monastery. When she stood in front of her father, he was amazed and had no doubt left: Marina was ready to join the monastery. He gave her a new name, Marin, this marked the beginning of a new chapter in her life. Marin, took all their belongings and gave them to the poor.

She helped many in need, and kept nothing for herself. She knew that Christians should always be ready to help the poor without asking for anything in return. Both Marin and her father went to the monastery, where they were welcomed and began their holy journey. Marin lived in the same monastic cell as her father, and they both focused their lives on Christ. After many years her father passed away, Marin refused to let sadness overwhelm her because she trusted in God's wisdom and promises

Marin lived a life of obedience, constant prayer and fasting. One day the bishop sent Marin and two other monks to a village nearby to serve the people there. It got dark quickly, so the monks agreed to spend the night in the village.

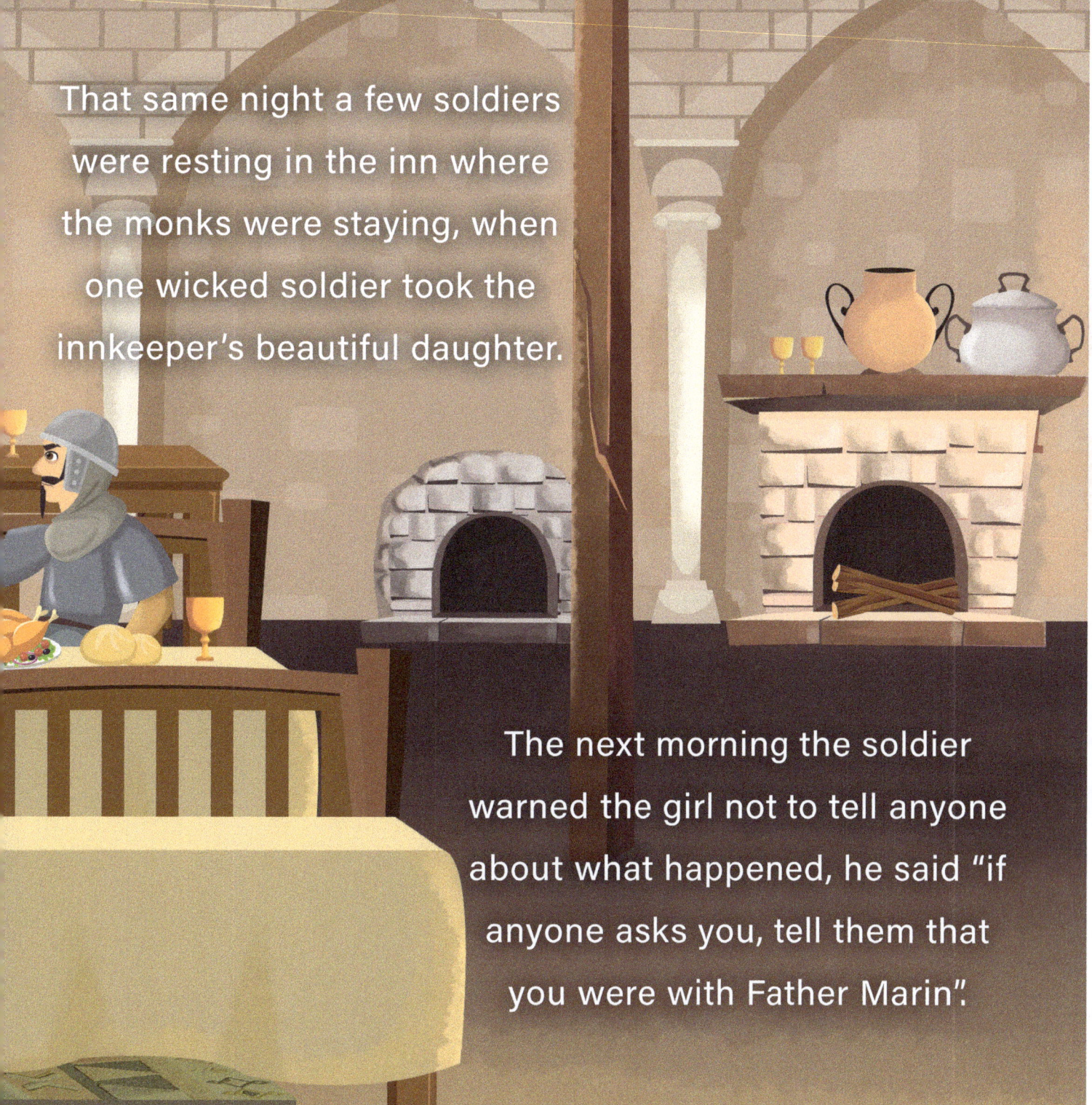

That same night a few soldiers were resting in the inn where the monks were staying, when one wicked soldier took the innkeeper's beautiful daughter.

The next morning the soldier warned the girl not to tell anyone about what happened, he said "if anyone asks you, tell them that you were with Father Marin".

After some time the innkeeper's daughter became pregnant and when her father asked how it happened? She remembered the soldier's warning and said "Father Marin is responsible for this". The innkeeper was furious, so he rushed to the monastery to meet the bishop and confront Father Marin. The bishop comforted the distressed innkeeper, he called for Father Marin and punished him. The Bishop was disappointed, he couldn't believe one of his monks would do this. In complete obedience, Father Marin fell to the ground and said "forgive me, I am young and I have sinned".

Father Marin did not argue because she knew God would look after her. She remembered in the bible it says "The righteous person may have troubles, but the Lord delivers him from them all" (Psalm 34:19). The bishop, seeking justice, cast out Father Marin from the monastery. She made a shelter in the wilderness nearby and lived there. When the innkeeper's daughter gave birth, she brought the baby to Father Marin. Father Marin continued to be the Lord's obedient servant and took the baby, she nursed him and fed him milk from animals nearby.

After some time the monks felt sorry for Father Marin, the bishop gave her permission to return but harsh rules were put in place for her to follow. She had to do all the cooking, cleaning and watering as well as the usual monastic duties while also caring for the baby. Father Marin's obedience allowed her to always stay focussed on God, being a humble and Christlike person. This virtue allowed her to know God, it gave her a taste of Heaven while she was in the desert. In the same way that Jesus' obedience allowed Him to conquer death, Father Marin's obedience allowed her to conquer anything that stood in the way of her relationship with God.

When the child grew up, he became a monk and obediently served God. Father Marin grew very old and one day passed away. In preparation for the funeral the bishop asked the monks to dress Father Marin in a new tunic. After removing her clothes the monks discovered that Father Marin was a woman. Feeling puzzled they quickly called the bishop and showed him what they discovered. The bishop was filled with sadness because he treated Father Marin harshly. He quickly summoned the innkeeper and explained that Father Marin was a woman, not a man. The innkeeper fell down on his knees lifting his hands in the air praying for Father Marin's forgiveness.

On the day of her funeral, a blind monk who had prayed for her intercession was healed. This was Saint Marina's first miracle. Soon after, the truth was revealed, the innkeeper's daughter and the soldier admitted what had happened. The innocent Saint Marina's Christlike obedience was revealed and praised by all. Through her, God performed many miracles. She is the perfect example of obedience, humility and courage as she followed God's commands every step of the way. Her actions teach us that to be obedient to God and our parents is not a weakness, it is to follow in Jesus' footsteps.

Saint Marina is the beloved intercessor of many.

THE END

www.ingramcontent.com/pod-product-compliance
Lightning Source LLC
Chambersburg PA
CBHW060856090426
42736CB00023B/3492